In Defense
of Latin
in the Mass

In Defense of Latin in the Mass

THE CASE FOR THE CHURCH'S TIMELESS LITURGICAL LANGUAGE

BY

POPE BENEDICT XIV

TRANSLATED BY

FR. ROBERT NIXON, OSB

FOREWORD BY

JOSEPH SHAW

TAN Books
Gastonia, North Carolina

Translated by Fr. Robert Nixon, OSB

Cover design by David Ferris—www.davidferrisdesign.com

Cover image: Ceremony held in the Cappella Paolina, Vatican by Francesco Piranesi, after Louis Jean Desprez, 1787. The Met Museum. Public Domain.

ISBN: 978-1-5051-2803-1
Kindle ISBN: 978-1-5051-2804-8
ePUB ISBN: 978-1-5051-2805-5

Published in the United States by
TAN Books
PO Box 269
Gastonia, NC 28053
www.TANBooks.com

Printed in India

*For all flesh is as grass; and all the glory thereof
as the flower of grass.
The grass is withered, and the flower thereof
is fallen away.
But the word of the Lord endureth for ever.*

—1 Peter 1:24–25

Contents

Foreword

THE ROMAN CHURCH has taken great care to preserve
Latin in her liturgy throughout the ages. Pope Benedict
XIV's defense of Latin in the liturgy is not an anomaly
but a link in a golden chain of such statements. Notable
among them are the Ecumenical Council of Trent in 1562
and Pope Pius VI in 1794,[1] when condemning the Jansenist Council of Pistoia. Latin's importance in the liturgy
continued to be reiterated well into the twentieth century,
notably by Pope Pius XII[2] and Pope John XXIII.[3]

Benedict XIV, however, goes into much greater detail
than these others. John XXIII, for example, was more
preoccupied by using Latin in seminary studies, paus-
ing only briefly to note that bishops should "be on their
guard" against those criticizing "the use of Latin in the
teaching of the higher sacred studies or in the Liturgy."
Pius XII, similarly, had merely dismissed vernaculariza-
tion as an "innovation." On the eve of the final assault
on the use of the Latin Church's ancient liturgical language, its defense was not well-articulated.

Benedict XIV's argument reverently starts from the
words of the Council of Trent, which states, baldly, "it

---

[1] In his bull *Auctorem Fidei*.

[2] In his encyclical *Mediator Dei* (1947), no. 59; cf. no. 108.

[3] In the apostolic constitution *Veterum Sapientia* (1962).

has not seemed expedient to the Fathers, that [the liturgy] should be every where celebrated in the vulgar tongue."[4]

Why has it not seemed expedient to the Fathers of the Council of Trent to have the Mass translated? Benedict XIV cites the overwhelming variety of vernacular languages: "Vernacular languages are not proper to nations and peoples alone, but differ significantly from city to city and village to village." The true pastoral care here should be noted: the attempt to provide a genuinely vernacular liturgy to Europeans in the sixteenth or eighteenth century would have been as impossible as the attempt to do so today in a country with a large number of dialects, such as Nigeria. In both cases, hundreds of vernaculars compete for attention, far exceeding the Church's resources in terms of translators or linguistically qualified priests. It is inevitable, indeed, that when the Missal is translated into African and other less well-known languages, it can end up being made not from the official Latin text but from another vernacular Missal, such as an English one: a translation of a translation. Even using this expedient, only a tiny minority of African languages are reached, leaving vast numbers of African Catholics to experience the Mass in the former colonial language.

Did the Protestant reformers, who condemned the Church for failing to provide the liturgy in the

---

4   Council of Trent, Session 22, Chapter V, 1562. Pope Benedict XIV does emphasize, however, that preaching should be done in the vernacular to explain the rites to the faithful.

language of the people, not care that their own liturgical books were incomprehensible to many of the less well-educated people for whom they were provided? It seems not. The English of Cranmer and the King James Bible, in a London/Kentish dialect larded with archaisms, must have been almost as incomprehensible for sixteenth-century speakers of Yorkshire dialect as it was for speakers of the Celtic languages then widely used in Cumbria, Wales, and Cornwall, not to mention Ireland and Scotland. As for the High German used by Luther, the language of the court, it was and has continued to be incomprehensible to many Germans.

The fact is that the Protestant reformers were engaged in an elite project, asserting the prerogatives of local elites against the international prestige and authority of the papacy.

It is often said that the Latin of the early Church was simply the language of the common people. This statement is inaccurate. The Vulgate Bible and liturgical Latin established a specialized sacred register with a distinct vocabulary replete with archaisms, new coinages, and idioms carried over from Hebrew and Greek. Furthermore, as Pope Benedict XIV points out, the Church made no attempt to translate the liturgy into the minority languages of the Western Roman Empire. He cites Saint Augustine on the widespread use in North Africa of Punic, once spoken by the Carthaginians. Indeed, there is evidence of persisting minority languages from many parts of the Western Empire, just

as there is of non-Greek speaking communities in the
East. Later, Saint Patrick introduced the Latin Mass to
Ireland while Saint Boniface brought it to Germany.
Latin eventually became incomprehensible to people
even within the old borders of the Roman Empire, and
the Council of Tours responded in the ninth century
(Pope Benedict reminds us) by commanding priests to
preach in the vernacular.

Practical considerations, such as the multiplicity of
vernacular languages, were not the only ones at the
root of the reluctance of the Latin Church to translate
the liturgy, even (as Pope Benedict emphasizes) in the
context of major new mission territories such as those
of the Slavs and the Chinese, despite acknowledging
that in principle vernacular liturgies are possible. The
deeper reason is only hinted at by Pope Benedict when,
considering the possibility that parish priests be tasked
with translating the Missal into local dialects, he re-
marks that "such a procedure would be totally absurd
and wholly unworthy of the dignity of the Mass."

Yes, it is about the dignity of the Mass.

It is not just a matter of the accuracy and stability
of the texts but of their "dignity" in a wider sense. The
Missal has a greater dignity and elicits greater reverence
in the worshipper if it is celebrated in a language which
is itself holy, set aside for sacred uses.

This point is elucidated in the other work included
in this volume, the text of the Franciscan Hierotheus
Confluentinus, who points out the value of Latin for

the "reverence and dignity" of the Mass. If it were in the vernacular, by contrast, he points out that worshippers would "regard this venerable Sacrament with less awe."

This debate over whether to use the vernacular or Latin in the liturgy is not trivial. It is of the deepest importance. It is not simply related to the Mass but has a connection intimately with our devotion to and worship of the Blessed Sacrament, the source and summit of our faith. It is interesting to see how the debate on the use of Latin has evolved over time, especially among the Petrine Office. It is an irony that the same man who most clearly wrote this point into the papal magisterium was also personally responsible for the almost complete disappearance of Latin as a liturgical language: Pope Paul VI. He remarked, in a general audience address, "The introduction of the vernacular will certainly be a great sacrifice for those who know the beauty, the power and the expressive sacrality of Latin. We are parting with the speech of the Christian centuries; we are becoming like profane intruders in the literary preserve of sacred utterance."[5]

Tragically, Pope Paul VI failed to see that a greater degree of word-by-word comprehension could not compensate for a decline of devotion, despite having made precisely this very argument in an earlier document. Specifically, his 1966 apostolic letter *Sacrificium Laudis*, which was addressed to religious superiors: "It

---

[5]   November 26, 1969.

is to be feared that the choral office would turn into a mere bland recitation, suffering from poverty and begetting weariness, as you yourselves would perhaps be the first to experience. One can also wonder whether men would come in such numbers to your churches in quest of the sacred prayer, if its ancient and native tongue, joined to a chant full of grave beauty, resounded no more within your walls."[6]

It is for us, half a century later, to deliver faithfully to future generations a liturgical tradition which gives the Church's inexpressibly sacred rites a language fitting to them, a language that, by its "concise, varied and harmonious style, full of majesty and dignity,"[7] vividly conveys to us the liturgy's beauty and grandeur.

Let us be edified, dear reader, by the words of our forefather in the faith, Pope Benedict XIV, and be enriched by the Roman Church's sacred language in furthering our reverence for the liturgy.

Joseph Shaw
President, Una Voce International,
and Chairman of the Latin Mass Society
(England and Wales)

---

[6]   Translation by Fr. Thomas Crean, OP.

[7]   Pope Pius XI, apostolic letter *Officiorum Omnium* (1922).

Translator's Note

POPE BENEDICT XIV (1675–1758), while unfamiliar to most contemporary Catholics, is a figure of immense importance in the post-Tridentine Church. Born to a noble family in Bologna, and baptized as Prospero Lorenzo Lambertini, he soon distinguished himself for his piety, humility, diplomacy, and scholarship. As a cardinal and pope, he was instrumental in implementing the reforms of Trent and reinvigorating Thomistic theology. As an author and scholar, he was, and still remains, far more prolific than any other pontiff in history, with his *Opera Omnia* filling many weighty tomes and being published in numerous editions.

Until now, his works have remained untranslated and inaccessible to Anglophone readers. The present short treatise is taken from his *De Sacrosancto Missae Sacrificio Libri tres* (Three Books on the Holy Sacrifice of the Mass). This highly influential and popular work was published in at least ten separate editions in the eighteenth and nineteenth centuries.

In these pages, Benedict XIV offers a convincing defense for the use of Latin as the normative liturgical language in the Mass of the Roman Catholic Church. Moreover, Benedict XIV was fully aware of the various dissenting opinions on this topic, which had arisen primarily as a result of the Protestant schism. Interestingly, the objections to the use of Latin in the liturgy in the eighteenth century differ very little from those which continue to be voiced in our own times. His responses are offered with unwavering charity and reasonableness, and are supported by his own vast erudition, keen insight, and detailed knowledge of the tradition and Church history.

In this booklet, the translator has added footnotes and short commentaries in order to clarify the arguments presented and to provide context which might not be obvious for the modern reader. Included also as an appendix is the essay on the use of Latin in the Mass by Hierotheus Confluentinus, the provincial of the Capuchin Franciscans in Germany (1682–1766). This magisterial discourse offers a clear summary of the reasons for the use of Latin in the liturgy and cogent responses to the most common objections to it. An introductory discussion of the question of the lawfulness of the continued use of Latin in the liturgy and the canonical status of the Missal of Pius V is also included.

In studying this work, it is important to note that the arguments and responses offered by the Holy Father, Pope Benedict XIV, are still valid since they emerge either from theological truth, history, or reason, all of which—like the sacred liturgy itself—are impervious to arbitrary and capricious alteration and to the changing fashions and passing trends of the times.

Fr. Robert Nixon, OSB
Abbey of the Most Holy Trinity
New Norcia, Western Australia

The Question of the Lawfulness of the Continued Use of Latin in the Liturgy, and the Canonical Status of the Missal of Saint Pius V

THE QUESTION OF the lawfulness of the continued use of Latin in the liturgy of the Roman Catholic Church may, at first glance, appear to be an uncomplicated one. A simplistic approach would be to say, "The pope is the supreme ruler of the Church. Therefore, whatever the current pope says on the matter answers the question. Rome has spoken—the question is answered!"

However, such an approach is not entirely satisfactory, nor accurate. For the pope himself exercises his power only in, and by virtue of, his communion with the other bishops of the Church (Canon 333§2). This communion, if it is to be complete, is necessarily both *synchronic*, embracing the college of bishops at any given time, and *diachronic*, embracing the college of bishops throughout all of history. This later aspect, diachronic communion, includes communion with his predecessors in the Petrine office, or, in other words, continuity with the rulings and determinations of previous popes.

For this reason, the pope himself is bound by the authentic and long-established traditions of the Church.

Any new decrees or decisions of the Church are necessarily interpreted through the lens of existing traditions, and also circumscribed by and contained within such traditions. A "hermeneutic of continuity" is thus always implicit, and, as Canon 25 states, "Consuetudo est optima legum interpres" (Custom is the best interpreter of the law).

Moreover, within the juridical model of the Roman Church, long-established practices and traditions are understood to have the status of law. Thus a new *motu proprio*, decree, or bull does not have the power to invalidate a long-established practice. This is expressed clearly and unequivocally in Canon 28: "Lex non revocat consuetudines centenarias aut immemorabiles" (The law does not revoke practices which are centuries old, or existing from times immemorial). It could be argued that the use of Latin in the liturgy of the Roman Catholic Church is perhaps the primary and most exemplary case of those venerable customs or practices which are "centenarias aut immemorabiles," and therefore not able to be revoked by a simple legislative act.

It is pertinent to note that the Roman Catholic Church is essentially identical with, and identifies itself canonically as, the *Ecclesia Latina* (the Latin Church) (Canon 1). It is therefore clear that to prohibit the use of Latin in the Roman Catholic (or Latin) Church would be, in a sense, to deny its very nature and identity. Indeed, the Second Vatican Council recognized this as a manifest fact, declaring that "linguae latinae usus, salvo particulari iure, in Ritibus latinis servetur" (the use of the Latin language, notwithstanding [any] particular right, is to be retained in the Latin rite). One might say that it is self-evident that the Church of the Latin rite (i.e., the Roman Catholic Church) should use Latin as its principal and normative liturgical language since this is constitutive of its identity. If it ceases to use Latin in this manner, it ceases *ipso facto* to be the "Latin Church." Of course, this does not exclude the use of the vernacular—but such use, however extensive it may be, always remains a permitted exception rather than a norm.

The issue of the canonical status of the Missal authorized by Pope Saint Pius V following the deliberations of the Council of Trent is one which is of some importance in the life of the contemporary Church. In the bull *Quo primum* issued on July 14, 1570, Saint Pius V declares unequivocally:

> In order that this Missal may be used in singing or reciting the Mass in any churches whatsoever without any scruple of conscience of fear or punishment, sentence or incursion of censure, we grant and concede, by our apostolic authority and according to the present tenor, that it may henceforth be followed in every respect, and may freely and lawfully be used—*indeed perpetually. . . . We simi-*

> *larly decree and declare that no one should be forced or*
> *coerced to alter this Missal, by any person whatsoever;*
> *and that this present decree cannot ever be revoked or*
> *modified, but shall forever remain valid and always*
> *stand in its full force.*

Can such permission and authorization to use the Tridentine Missal, once granted in a manner which is so expressly and emphatically perpetual and irrevocable, ever be validly or meaningfully rescinded? Was Saint Pius V perhaps somehow speaking prophetically when he wrote the above lines?

This question calls for much deep and serious reflection in our present, troubled times. May the Spirit of Truth guide us.

IN DEFENSE OF LATIN IN THE MASS

(taken from *De Sacrosancto Missae Sacrificio Libri tres*)

by Pope Benedict XIV

1

A refutation of the view that the Mass being celebrated in Latin prevents the faithful from understanding its meaning

Translator's Commentary

Pope Benedict XIV here notes that the use of Latin is the norm and consistent practice of the Western Church, which is essentially synonymous with the Latin Rite of the Catholic Church, or the Roman Catholic Church. He notes that the objection to Latin on the grounds that it prevents the faithful from understanding the meaning of the liturgy is specious. On the contrary, he points out that the Council of Trent has specifically directed all priests to provide instruction and explanations in the course of the liturgy so that the faithful may be fully aware of the sacred actions' meaning. If this directive of Trent is adhered to by priests, the objection of the difficulty in understanding is unfounded.

~~~

As FAR AS language is concerned, in the Western Church, the Mass is celebrated in Latin. It is a most presumptuous and impudent calumny, often uttered by those who object to the Latin Mass, that this practice results in the people not understanding or appreciating the liturgy.

The fact that this contention is false is clearly demonstrated by the Council of Trent. For in Session XXII, *On the Sacrifice of the Mass,* chapter VIII, the fathers of the council mandated that:

> Although the Mass contains within itself great instruction for the people, it does not appear to the council fathers that it is fitting for it to be celebrated in the vernacular. On the contrary, the ancient rites of the Church—as approved and practiced by the Holy Roman Church, which is the mother and teacher of all others—are to be retained. But, lest the sheep of Christ should be left hungry, and the children be deprived of bread while there is no one to break open the mysteries of the Faith for them, this holy synod decrees to all pastors and those with the care of souls that they should frequently explain those things which are read in the Mass. They should do this within the celebration of the Mass itself, either themselves or through others. Especially on Sundays and feast days, they should endeavor to expound the mystery of the most holy sacrifice of the Mass.

2

Pasquier Quesnel's advocacy of the Mass in the vernacular refuted by the consensus of bishops, and by authoritative scholars

Translator's Commentary

Pasquier Quesnel (1634–1791) was a French theologian aligned with the heretical (or heterodox) Jansenist movement. He published over one hundred theological and liturgical propositions. Among these propositions was the view that preventing the population from joining their voices with the liturgy was contrary to apostolic practice and contrary to the will of God. The implication of this was that the use of Latin unfairly excluded congregational participation in the Mass (a similar argument used by contemporary advocates of vernacular language in the Mass). Benedict XIV, to show that Quesnel's propositions cannot be treated with credibility or accepted, points out that Pope Clement XI condemned them (including specifically those relating to the use of the vernacular) in his apostolic constitution

Unigenitus. In this, Clement XI declares, ex cathedra, that Quesnel's propositions, including those on the use of the vernacular in the liturgy, are:

> Condemned as false, misleading, evil-sounding, offensive to pious ears, scandalous, pernicious, rash, injurious to the Church and her practice, insulting not only to the Church but also the secular powers, seditious, impious, blasphemous, and influenced by heresy itself; and, besides, favoring heretics and heresies, and also schisms, erroneous, close to heresy, many times condemned, and finally heretical, clearly renewing many heresies respectively and most especially those which are contained in the infamous propositions of Jansen, and indeed accepted in that sense in which these have been condemned.

He also cites the determination of the bishops of France, as well as leading Catholic theologians of the time.

———— ✄ ————

AMONG THE PROPOSITIONS of Quesnel which Pope Clement XI condemned in his bull *Unigenitus*, the eighty-sixth was: "To deprive the common people of the solace of joining their voices to that of the Church is contrary to both the practice of the apostles and the will of God." The sense of this condemned proposition of Quesnel is manifold, but included a pernicious notion that Quesnel fervently wished to propagate—namely, that the Mass should only be celebrated in the vernacular tongue. No less than one hundred French bishops understood this to be Quesnel's intention, and they condemned him accordingly in their pastoral document on this question. Moreover, [Fulvio] Fontana[8] of the Society of Jesus, a man outstanding both for erudition and piety, similarly understood this to be Quesnel's meaning and intent, and refuted him convincingly and conclusively, in chapter V of his book against Quesnel's propositions. Similarly, [Fulgenzio] Belleli,[9] the illustrious theologian of the Order of Hermits of Saint Augustine, also refutes Quesnel's contention regarding the celebration of the Mass in the vernacular in his outstanding book *On Saint Augustine's understanding of the reparation of human nature after the first fall.*

---

8   Fulvio Fontana, SJ (1648–1723), was a highly regarded and prolific theological author of the time.

9   Fulgenzio Belleli, a leading theologian of the time, who became prior general of the Augustinian order. The refutation of Belleli is based on the observation that "participation" for those attending liturgies does not primarily mean communal verbalizing of the texts of the prayer, but is rather more properly understood to be of a spiritual or mental nature. He cites texts from the Church Fathers, and in particular Saint Augustine, which show that it was the consistent practice in the early Church for ordained ministers to offer prayer on behalf of the entire Church, with congregations joining the spiritual intentions (but not their physical voices) with this prayer.

3

A refutation of arguments for vernacular liturgy based on isolated and particular historical precedents

Translator's Commentary

Pope Benedict XIV here acknowledges the published observation of François de Rouxel de Médavy (1604–91), archbishop of Rouen (a city in France), that there was strong evidence that Mass was celebrated in the vernacular in certain locations in his archdiocese in the remote past. The Holy Father does not enter into the question of the historical veracity of this view, apart from noting that it is disputed by many authorities while it is accepted by others. However, Pope Benedict XIV does indicate that even if something may have been previously practiced by the Church in particular situations—such as the use of the vernacular in the liturgy, or the imposition of harsh, physical penances—it does not necessarily validate its reinstatement at the present time. If the Church is empowered to permit the use of the vernacular in certain times and circumstances, it is evidently also necessarily empowered to rescind such permission.

8

If the Church can, in particular cases, allow for exceptions to the use of Latin in the liturgy, it is evident that such cases are, by their very nature, exceptions rather than the norm. Indeed, the fact that Latin remains the norm for the liturgy of the Roman Catholic Church and the use of the vernacular an exception to be permitted in particular cases is explicitly rearticulated at the most recent ecumenical council in *Sacrosanctum Concilium* 36§1.

⁓

[FRANÇOIS DE ROUXEL de Médavy,] bishop of Rouen, in his *Manuale*, writes that it has been amply proven that it was an ancient custom in the Church in his diocese for Mass sometimes to be celebrated in the vernacular language. He further states that [at the time] such a practice made the celebration accessible to all so that each one could prepare his soul for the Eucharistic sacrifice. Many have held this statement to be dubious and unsubstantiated. There are, however, some who defend this finding. Yet, even if it is true, it does not follow that the practice of saying the Mass in a language which all members of the congregation may not necessarily understand is wrong.

[The fact that the use of the vernacular may have been the practice in certain places in earlier times is not a valid argument against the use of Latin now.] Such an argument would be like saying that Christians were more easily deterred from sinning in the remote past when sins were often punished with long, painful, and arduous [physical] penances, and that therefore the current, more moderate approach to penances is wrong. [The fact that such things may have their usefulness in a particular time and place is not an argument for mandating them universally.]

Here it is well to consult the author of the tract *The Optimal Manner of Hearing the Mass*, published in Paris in 1680.[10] In chapter VI of this work, the author wisely observes that just as at that time and place the Church judged it more useful for the souls of the faithful and more effective in converting them from their sinful ways of life for the Mass to be celebrated in the vernacular and to impose grave [physical] penances, so now, for just and serious causes and having considered the wisest available advice, the same Church is able to require that the Mass be celebrated in the traditional language of Latin, even if it is no longer understood by all, and to remit the types of penances which were formerly imposed. The one Church—which deemed it best in some particular circumstances and times for the vernacular to be permitted if it helped people to receive the Eucharist worthily, and which deemed it best for harsh penalties to be imposed to deter people from sinning—must necessarily have the power of revoking this permission and establishing a discipline which it, in its wisdom, finds now to be more fruitful in achieving the same holy goals.

---

[10]   Benedict XIV does not state the author of this work in his text. However, it is almost certain that he is referring to *De la meilleure manière d'entendre la Sainte Messe* by Nicolas Le Tourneux, which was published in Paris in 1680.

4

A demonstration that Latin has been used in the liturgy of the Western Church since the earliest times

Translator's Commentary

Pope Benedict XIV presents compelling evidence to show that Latin was the language used in the Western Church since apostolic times. He cites leading Church historians to support this view. Moreover, he argues that a particular sentence in one of Augustine's letters, which was sometimes used to support the opinion that the Punic language was used in the African Church, has been often misread and contends, on the contrary, that Augustine's writings prove that Latin was the language of the entire Western Church, even in Roman Africa. The point of establishing this is that it demonstrates that the liturgy of the Western, or Roman, Catholic Church has been Latin consistently since the earliest times, and even in the most remote localities of the Western Empire.

~ ∽ ~

THE LEARNED THEOLOGIAN Johannes Eck[11] has written extensively against the Lutherans, who disapprove of our practice of celebrating the Mass in Latin. He opines, in a homily given in 1523, that the apostles and their successors celebrated the Mass in the Hebrew language until the time of the emperor Hadrian,[12] and from that time Greek began to be used in the sacred rites [and Latin began to be used shortly thereafter]. There are many who believe that no languages other than Latin, Greek, or Hebrew were used in the sacred liturgy in memory of the three languages in which the title of the Lord was written on the inscription on the cross.

But the most expert ecclesiastical historians, who have investigated the matter deeply, maintain that the apostles and their successors not only preached but celebrated the divine liturgies in the languages of the people to whom they were bringing the Gospel. Therefore, in the Western Church, the Latin language was uniformly used, which at the time in question was the vernacular language common to all in the Western Empire. One may consult [Cardinal Giovanni] Bona, *Rerum Liturgicarum,* Book 1, chapter IV, number 4; Bocquillot, *Liturgiae,* Book 1, chapter XI; Le Brun, Volume 4, p. 201; and Martene, *De Antiquis Ecclesiae Ritibus,* Book 1, chapter III, article 3.

But to some, Augustine's *Letter 74* to Bishop Novatus is held to contradict [the view that Latin was used

---

[11] A German theologian (1486–1543) who wrote polemic works against Luther.
[12] AD 76–138.

exclusively in the Western Church in the apostolic and patristic age]. In that letter, Augustine writes that he has retained his brother, the deacon Lucillus, in his house because he [Lucillus] knows the Latin language, and that few others in that region who know it are to be found. The text cited [by those who seek to prove that Latin was not used in the North African Church] is: *Sed cum Latina lingua, cujus inopia in nostris regionibus evangelica dispension multum laborat.*[13] But all must see that the text here is confused or corrupted, for there is nothing to which the words *Latina lingua* may be sensibly connected. Therefore, a more correct reading of the text would appear to be: *Sed cum punicae linguage inopia, in nostris regionibus Evangelicae dispensatio multum laboret.*[14] And this reading is fully consistent with what Augustine says in his *Sermon 176* (numbered by others as Sermon 24) on the words of the apostle, delivered to the people of Hippo. In this sermon, he announces, "I speak to you in Latin, because not all of you know the Punic language." And we have many texts from the same holy Doctor [Augustine] out of which it is clearly established that Latin literary studies flourished in [Roman] Africa, and that it was the common language of all [in that region.]

---

[13] The sense of this sentence is unclear, and its syntax is somewhat faulty, as Benedict XIV points out.

[14] "Because of the poverty (i.e., limitations in concepts and vocabulary) of the Punic language (one of the native languages of northern Africa), the spread of the Gospel in our regions (i.e., northern Africa) is a laborious task."

5

The problems associated with the variability and disunity of vernacular speech, and its constant mutations through time

Translator's Commentary

The variability of vernacular language from one locality to another and its constant variations through time are identified as grave impediments to its use as a liturgical language. The author argues that the use of the vernacular, with its semantic and cultural fluidity, would give rise to innumerable uncertainties about the true meaning of the liturgy.

～⌢～

BUT THE QUESTION [of whether or not Latin was used consistently in the Western Church since the earliest times] is not, perhaps, the critical hinge of the controversy. It is asked by some that if the liturgy in the early [Western] Church was said in Latin, which was the common or vernacular language of the time—but now is known only by educated people—should it not now be said in what is the common language at the present time? The Catholic Church has consistently vehemently opposed such a step. This question was considered thoroughly—and the proposition definitively refuted—in the pastoral letter of Jacques Golbert, bishop of Rouen (contained in the collection of documents of provincial councils for that diocese, p. 172).

Is there anyone of sound mind who would recommend that because there are so many vernacular idioms and local dialects, parish priests and preachers should be permitted to translate the Latin texts of the Mass into the local tongue themselves as they celebrate the liturgy? Such a procedure would be totally absurd and wholly unworthy of the dignity of the Mass.

[But such a procedure would be necessary because] vernacular languages are not proper to nations and peoples alone but differ significantly from city to city and village to village. And as successive years pass by, any vernacular language is constantly changing and in fluctuation. Indeed, this mutation of meaning even happened in Latin itself [when it was the vernacular language], as Polybius relates in Book 3 [of his *History of the Punic Wars*]. He described how a treaty made for peace at the end of the first Punic war was no longer able to be understood with any certainty by the conclusion of the second Punic war.

In whatever mutation of meaning or sense there is in a language, six hundred occasions for contention and disagreement inevitably arise! And even if the people were able to understand separately each individual word of the Mass in their vernacular language, there would not necessarily be consistent comprehension as to its overall sense. Hence an infinite number of errors and misapprehensions would spring up.

6

Examples of the retention of the ancient idioms as liturgical languages by the Israelites and the Greeks

Translator's Commentary

Pope Benedict XIV points out that in two major and ancient religious traditions—namely, those of the Hebrews and the Greeks—the liturgy was originally celebrated in what was formerly the vernacular language. But, in the course of time, these vernacular languages (Hebrew and koine Greek) came to be supplanted by new idioms in the speech of the general population. Nevertheless, both of these traditions chose to retain the older and original form of language in their liturgy. There is an evident analogy between the use of Hebrew in Jewish worship and koine Greek in the liturgy of the Greek Church, with the continuing use of Latin in the Western Church.

Many other similarly analogous cases abound, such as the use of the Coptic language in the Coptic Churches, the use of Syriac in the Syriac Church of the East, and even the use of classical Arabic in Islam. The practice of having a sacral language different from the colloquial idiom is thus one which is common to all major traditions, and not a particular idiosyncrasy of the Roman Catholic Church.

~⁓~

EVEN THOUGH IT is sufficiently clear that the Mass ought not to be generally converted into vernacular languages, nevertheless it is significant [to consider some other examples which support the retention of Latin as our liturgical language in the West].

[Firstly, we may consider the example of the Hebrew people.] Until the time of their captivity in Babylon, the sacred language of the Hebrew people was identical to their everyday spoken idiom. The liturgy was therefore celebrated in a language originally understood by all. But at the time of the Babylonian exile, little by little knowledge of the original Hebrew language was lost to the common people, and they came to speak a dialect of Chaldean or Syriac instead. But once the exile was over and the Jewish people had returned to Israel, the Hebrew language continued to be most reverently used for sacred liturgy.

And there is surely no one who does not realize that the Greek [of the New Testament times] differs greatly from the idiom which modern Greeks speak today. The older form of Greek, which at one time was the vernacular, is now understood only by a highly educated minority. Nevertheless, the older form of Greek is still diligently retained in the liturgy [of the Greek Church].

These venerable examples offer clear demonstrations that it is neither necessary nor desirable for the language of the sacred liturgy to be brought into line with contemporary vernacular, or a language which is understood both by the educated and the less literate. Although the language of the liturgy [in the case of the Hebrews and the Greeks] was originally identical with the common vernacular, little by little it became a sacral idiom which only an educated minority understood. [The retention of the Latin in the Western Church is a practice which is exactly analogous to these other traditions.]

7

The dangers of dissention, disunity, and schism resulting from alterations in the language of the sacred liturgy

Translator's Commentary

Pope Benedict XIV recalls the reactions to a publication of the missal translated into French in the year 1660. It aroused widespread concern amongst the clergy, who believed that it would give rise to error and schism in the French church. They expressed their concerns to Pope Alexander VII, who promptly banned the publication. The royal government of France also refused to give publication of the translated missal, considering that it would give rise to social disunity and religious error.

THERE IS A very real peril that many errors that are harmful to the harmony of the Church and to the unity of the Faith may arise from changes in the language of the sacred liturgy. This was amply proven in the case of the missal translated into the French tongue, which Father Vois, of the Order of Preachers, published in

1660.[15] In response to this novelty, the French clergy
vehemently, and almost unanimously, objected to the
missal. They feared that this publication would give rise
to numerous errors, scandals, and dissensions. Indeed,
history has shown that this fear was well justified!

The French clergy accordingly raised its grave concerns and fears with the pontiff of the time, Pope Alexander VII, and formally complained about the publication of the translation. And the Holy Father, in
response to these concerns, condemned the publication
in the following year. Nor did the book ever obtain
authorization or permission for publication from the
French crown, the provision of which was, indeed, prohibited by papal decree.

The whole incident is related, with relevant documents, in the compilation *Criticorum Sacrorum*, Volume 4, p. 583, and by [Fulvio] Fontana in his work
against the propositions of Quesnel, Volume 3, p. 916,
and in the previously cited work by Belleli, Volume 2.[16]

---

[15]   It has not been possible to locate a copy of this publication, or to
find further details of its author.
[16]   The book referred to here is cited towards the end of chapter 2 of
the present work.

8

The unanimous acceptance of Latin as a liturgical language in the Western Church throughout the entire Middle Ages

Translator's Commentary

Here Pope Benedict XIV presents what he believes is the strongest argument for the continued use of Latin in the sacred liturgies—namely, that it has been in use in the Western Church since the very beginning. Moreover, by the early Middle Ages, Latin was no longer a vernacular language, yet it continued to be used in the liturgy of the Church—without any objections ever being raised—throughout the entire Middle Ages, that is, for virtually one thousand years.

WE NOW ARRIVE at the most powerful and undisputable argument in this matter. As we have already observed and demonstrated, it is clear that in the Western Church, the apostles and their successors celebrated the Mass in the Latin language. At those times, Latin was the common idiom for all the people in that region.

But this Latin language gradually underwent various mutations. In Italy, by about the seventh or eighth century, it had transformed itself into a form of vernacular speech, [that is, a language which was identifiable as Italian rather than Latin.[17]] The Goths had invaded Italy at the beginning of the fifth century, under their king, Alaric. In the middle of this same century, the Huns also invaded, under Attila; and the Vandals, under Genseric. But it was not primarily these invasions which caused the transformation of the Latin language in Italy.

Rather, it is to the invasion of Italy by the Heruli[18] [and the events which followed] that the change of language may be principally attributed. These, under the leadership of Odoacer, dominated the length and breadth of Italy, and the Romans acclaimed Odoacer as the king of their nation. Following this, the Goths seized power, under the command of Theodoric. Once Odoacer was deposed, this Theodoric was declared to be king of Italy by the emperor at the time, Zeno. After a further sixty years had elapsed and the Goths had been expelled from the Italian peninsula, the reign of Italy was restored once more to the august emperor Justinian Caesar.

---

[17] Of course, the evolution of Latin into the various Romance languages (Italian, Spanish, French, etc.) was a gradual process. But it is agreed by scholars that by the seventh or eighth centuries, the transformation was great enough to make the vernacular idioms recognizable as distinct languages from Latin. At this stage, of course, Latin continued to be used in liturgy (as well as in law and for other more formal purposes).

[18] A tribe of Germanic people, possibly of Scandinavian origin.

From around the middle of the sixth century, the Lombards arose from the northern parts [of Europe]. These invaded and conquered Italy and ruled it for some 205 years, with some twenty-three different Lombard kings occupying the Italian throne in succession. But their domination of Italy was eventually overthrown by Charlemagne [the first Holy Roman emperor], who completed the campaign that was begun by his father [Pepin]. He compelled the Lombards into the region now known as Lombardy, and having put their armies to flight, he took their king, Desiderius, to France in captivity.

The origin of the Italian language may be attributed to all the above-described events and the long-enduring domination of the Lombards. This Italian vernacular idiom sprang from a progressive degeneration or deterioration of the Latin language. The original, pure form of the Latin language continued to be used in the writings and disputations of those who were literate and educated, but ceased to be the common idiom of everyday speech.

Now if this transformation of the Latin tongue took place in Italy, which may be described as the very home of that language, one may easily imagine how similar mutations were occurring during the same period throughout the other regions of the West, where colonists [who had originally spoken pure Latin] had resided since the early days of the Roman Empire.

Lest I digress excessively, it will suffice to cite canon 17 of the Council of Tours,[19] held at the beginning of the ninth century. This canon instructed priests and bishops, who were still in the practice of preaching in the Latin language, to use the vernacular tongue, rather than Latin [in giving homilies and sermons]. The instruction in question reads: "[All those involved in the ministry of preaching] should endeavor to give their homilies in the *Romana rustica* or German (*Teodisca*) so that what is preached may be more easily understood by all the faithful." The term *Romana rustica* refers to an idiom which was the vernacular language in France at the time, conflated out of several languages [namely, mutated Latin and local indigenous languages]. The term "German" (*Teodisca*) refers to the common language of the Germanic peoples. It was widely known in France at the time, which was then under the domination of Germanic kings. Out of this historical narration [and the cited canon], it is clearly evident that Latin had already long ceased to be the vernacular idiom in Western Europe.

And, notwithstanding the indisputable fact that Latin was no longer understood as a vernacular language, the Mass continued consistently to be celebrated in that language. And no one in the Church, for the space of so very many centuries [from the seventh or eighth century until the sixteenth century], ever raised any complaints about this practice, or stirred up the populace

---

[19] A city in France.

against it. The fact [that Latin was used in the Mass, despite it not being the common language, for almost one thousand years] and not a single objection was raised against it (except in very recent times) gives to this practice an immense and unshakeable weight of authority.

And we judge this vast weight of historical authority to be sufficient cause to reprove those who now presume to vituperate and cleave apart the holy Catholic Church with curses, on the grounds [of simply continuing to do what has been its consistent and universally accepted practice for virtually a millennium].

9

The particular and complex instance of the Slavonic liturgy, and the miraculous voice heard by Pope Hadrian II and the College of Cardinals

Translator's Commentary

Pope Benedict XIV here examines the question of the use of the vernacular language in the liturgy amongst the Slavonic people, especially during the initial stages of their conversion to the faith by Saint Cyril and Saint Methodius. At certain points, the use of the vernacular was deemed to be expedient or necessary, especially when there were not enough priests available with sufficient literacy to celebrate the Mass in Latin. Yet even then, the decision to permit the use of the Slavonic language was only a concession granted to address a particular necessity. In due course, when the number of educated candidates for the priesthood increased, permission to use the vernacular language in the Mass was revoked, and the Roman Catholic Church in the Slavonic countries came to adopt the universal norm of

the Latin Church—that is, of using Latin in the celebration of the Mass.

~⁓~

IT IS TO be acknowledged that grave challenges exist
when efforts are being made to convert a people to the
Faith for the first time. The question then often arises if
the liturgy should be translated into the local vernacular to facilitate the missionary efforts. During the time
of Pope Nicholas I, who was elevated to the pontificate
in the year 858, two Eastern monks who were brothers, Saint Cyril and Saint Methodius, began missionary
work to the Slavonic peoples. [This work was largely
successful.] The two brothers then travelled to Rome
in order to be consecrated as bishops so that they could
assume pastoral responsibility for the faithful in the
newly established churches.

But before they had arrived in Rome, Pope Nicholas
passed away. This was in the year 867. Hadrian II was
then elected as his successor. This new pontiff summoned
Cyril and Methodius to his presence to examine them
on their activities. For he had been informed that they
had introduced the Slavonic language into the liturgy of
the Church within their missionary territories. The two
brothers admitted to this, but they strenuously defended
themselves. And then followed a most wondrous incident, which is related by Aeneas Silvius [Piccolomini][20]
in chapter 13 of his *Historia Bohemica*. He writes:

---

[20] Aeneas Silvius Piccolomini was elected to the papacy, as Pope Pius II,

It is recorded that Cyril, when he was in Rome, besought the permission of the Roman pontiff that he should be able to use the Slavonic language for the conduct of divine liturgy, for the people whom he had baptized in that region. While the matter was being discussed by the sacred Senate [i.e., the College of Cardinals], there were many who raised objections, and much contradiction. But then a voice was heard by the whole assembly, as if coming from heaven, saying, "Let every spirit praise the Lord, and let all tongues declare their faith in him!"[21] And therefore, Cyril was granted an indult [for the use of the Slavonic language in the liturgy in the missionary territories].

But in the year 872, John VIII, having been made pope, directed Saint Methodius to cease to celebrate the Mass in the Slavonic language. He sent a letter to him, through Paul, the bishop of Buda,[22] which read as follows:

> We have heard indeed, that Masses are being sung in the barbaric tongue—that is, in the Slavonic language. Hence, through this letter directed to you

---

in 1458. Before his election to the pontifical see, he had acquired very considerable eminence as a man of letters and learning.

[21] Cf. Psalm 150:6, Philippians 2:11.

[22] The ancient capital of the Kingdom of Hungary.

through Paul, bishop of Buda, we hereby prohibit
you to celebrate the sacred solemnities of the Mass
in any language other than Latin or Greek, as is
the practice of the Church of God throughout the
entire world. However, we do permit you to preach
in the language of the local people.

But shortly afterwards, he reconsidered his decision and
revoked the prohibition of Methodius celebrating the
Mass in the Slavonic language, provided that the translation was faithful to the Latin. The Gospel was to be
read firstly in Latin, and then a translation into Slavonic could be provided for the benefit of the congregation.
Nevertheless, the pontiff explicitly indicated that it remained preferable for the Mass itself to be celebrated in
Latin. [He wrote thus:]

There is nothing, purely from the point of view
of faith or doctrine, which prevents Masses being
[validly] celebrated in the Slavonic language or the
holy Gospels or readings from the Old and New
Testaments being read in this language, on the condition that they are well and accurately translated.
Similarly, the other divine offices may also be [val-
idly] conducted in these languages. For the God
who created the three principal languages—Hebrew, Greek, and Latin—also created all others, to
His praise and glory. We command, nevertheless,

that in all the churches in your territories, in order
to show fitting reverence and honor, the Gospel be
read first in Latin. Following this, it may be read in
the Slavonic language if the congregation is unable
to understand Latin. This is in accordance with a
custom which is already seen to prevail in certain
churches [in your region]. And, if it is more pleas-
ing to you and your counsellors, we instruct and
advise that the Mass should be celebrated in Latin.

The pontiff here observes that it was then a custom in
certain churches for the Gospel to be read firstly in Latin, and afterwards in Slavonic. Indeed, it is indubita-
ble that it has been an ancient practice for the readings
from the Gospel, prophets, and Epistles to be read in
two languages. Certainly, in the [early] Roman Church
on certain days the readings from the Old Testament,
the Epistles, and the Gospels were read in both Greek
and Latin. Even today, when the pope is celebrating
solemnly, the Epistle is firstly read in Latin and then in
Greek, by the subdeacon. Similarly, the Gospel is firstly
read in Latin, and then sung by the deacon in Greek.

[It is interesting to refer to the work of] Thomasinus
[de Ferraria, OP], where he shows that, in the ninth
century, it was the practice in more solemn Masses in
the churches in Rome for the Epistle and Gospel to be
read firstly in Greek and then in Latin afterwards; while
in the churches in Constantinople, the Epistle and Gospel were read firstly in Latin, and then in Greek. This

custom was intended to signify the unity of the Latin and the Byzantine churches.

But to return to the Slavonic Mass, from which we have digressed somewhat, it is clear that there was a certain uncertainty and hesitation about it from the very beginning. For the legate of Alexander II—who was elected pope in 1061—declared in a council of the bishops of Dalmatia and Croatia that no one should henceforth presume to celebrate the divine mysteries in any languages other than Latin or Greek, and that the practice of using Slavonic in the sacred liturgy was to be abandoned. And Pope Gregory VII, in the year 1080, wrote a letter to Vladislav, king of Bohemia,[23] in which he urges him not to partake in communion with those who are excommunicated [by the Roman Church], nor to permit the sacred liturgies to be celebrated in the Slavonic language [within his kingdom].

---

[23]   From the date of this letter and the times of the papacy of Gregory VII, it seems likely that Hungary, rather than Bohemia, is actually intended here and that the king in question was (Saint) Ladislaus I.

10

The controversy regarding the use of the Chinese language in Masses in missionary territories of China, and the Church's decision against this practice

Translator's Commentary

Here the more recent case of the liturgy in the missionary territories of China is considered. It is shown that after careful deliberation, the Church determined that Latin was to be retained in the sacred rites.

AT THE BEGINNING of the previous century,[24] the question was raised of the use of the local vernacular language in the celebration of the divine liturgies within the Empire of China. Permission to use the Chinese vernacular was formally requested from the Holy See by the Missionary Faculty of the Society of Jesus. And the pontiff at the time, Pope Paul V, decreed, on January 25, 1615, that it should be permitted for the Mass and

---

[24] That is, the beginning of the seventeenth century.

other sacred liturgies to be celebrated in Chinese for the faithful of that nationality in the missionary territories of China. His letter extending this permission was dispatched but was never actually received by the missionaries in that region who had requested it.[25] A little later, a number of French bishops visited China, and at that time the request for formal permission from the Holy See to use the vernacular language in the liturgy was resubmitted [since the earlier letter granting permission had never arrived].

In this instance, a meeting was convened [to consider the request], attended by learned cardinals and prelates, as well as a number of distinguished theologians. Amongst their number was Father Christian Lupus.[26] The deliberations and decisions are related by Cardinal [Franciscus] Albitius in his work *De Inconstantia in Fide*, part 1, chapter 34. In the end, no decree granting the requested permission was granted.

In 1681, a missal translated into the Chinese language was sent to Pope Innocent XI for his consideration. Shortly afterwards, Father Philip Couplet, the procurator general of Missions to China, betook himself to see the pontiff in the hopes of obtaining his approval for the missal and permission for its use. However, he failed to obtain this approval from the pope. They then returned to France and there wrote a dissertation

---

[25] Presumably, it was lost in transit.

[26] Christian Lupus (1612–81), an important Flemish theologian and Augustinian priest.

on the usefulness of the translation, if its use were to be permitted. The principal arguments and chapters of this dissertation are included in the *Propylaeum [ad Acta Sanctorum]* for the month of May, in the same place where Nicholas I, Hadrian II, and John VIII are spoken of.[27] [Despite this dissertation, permission to use the Chinese language in the celebration of the Mass itself was not finally granted.]

---

[27] Presumably, its inclusion in the volume mentioned, and in relation to the lives of these popes, was based on the apparent parallel between the question of the use of Slavonic in the liturgy which took place under those pontiffs and the question of the use of the vernacular in the liturgy by missionaries in China.

11

Conclusions

It is to be concluded, therefore, that the constant and firm discipline of the Roman Catholic Church is for the language of the Mass not to be changed and not to be translated into the vernacular. Rather, the Mass is to be celebrated in the Latin language in which it was celebrated from the very beginning [of the Roman Church], even if this language has fallen out of colloquial use and is known only by an educated minority.

It remains, however, the prerogative of the Holy See to permit or prohibit the use of the local vernacular in the celebration of the sacred liturgies in those places where a people are newly converted to the Faith, as circumstances demand. But it is able to be asserted that the Holy See is more likely to select [candidates for sacred ministries] in those areas who show sufficient aptitude and to instruct them in the Latin language rather than granting permission for the celebration of the Mass in the vernacular idiom. This approach is comparable to what Saint Otho, bishop of Bamberg and apostle of Pomerania, who died in 1139, was accustomed to say to those who were newly converted to the Faith:

I urge and invite you—for I ought not to compel you—that, with your young men who are committed to studies for the sacred ministries, you should firstly instruct them in liberal studies [of Latin language and literature]. In this way, you—like other nations—will be able to have priests and clergy from your own people who are expert in Latin.

There are certain people who raise what is written in 1 Corinthians 14 as an objection to what we have said thus far. [In this passage, Saint Paul writes:]

If I come to you speaking in tongues, how shall I profit you, unless I speak to you some revelation, knowledge, prophecy, or doctrine? . . . If the trumpet sounds an uncertain note, who shall prepare themselves for battle? And similarly, if you speak with a tongue which is not comprehensible, how shall the assembly know what it is which is being said? You will be talking, so to speak, to the air!

Some contend that this passage demonstrates that the Mass should be celebrated only in the common language of the people. But this argument is specious and erroneous. For Saint Paul is here speaking specifically of the gift of tongues [glossolalia or knowledge of unknown languages]. He is [not speaking of the celebration of the divine liturgy itself] but simply urging persons who possess the gift of tongues not to use sermons

and speeches to the congregation as a means of osten-
tatiously displaying their charism but rather to address
them modestly in a language which is known to all.

Appendix

On the Language of the Celebration of the Mass

by Hierotheus Confluentinus, OFM Cap
from *Tractatus bipartitus de sacrosancto Missae sacrificio* (1759)

THE MASS IS not, as a general norm, to be celebrated in the vernacular language. Thus the Council of Trent unequivocally declared, offering a response to the contemporary anti-Catholics who pertinaciously maintain that it is not only fitting but even necessary for the Mass to be celebrated in the vernacular tongue. Such people insist that all of those present should understand, on a word-for-word basis, the sacrifice which is made in the presence of God. To Catholics, I shall offer [three] arguments [showing that it is fitting for the Mass to be celebrated in Latin].

The first argument is that if it was necessary to celebrate the Mass in the vernacular, the Catholic Church—which is the Church of Christ—spread throughout different regions and nations, would not be able to communicate with itself in its rites and sacramental actions. A German priest would not be able to celebrate in

France, nor a French priest in Germany, nor a Hungarian priest in Italy. For this reason alone, it is indispensable that the principal rite of divine worship (namely, the holy sacrifice of the Mass) should be celebrated in a single language known by the ministers of the Church throughout the entire world. And it would similarly be absurd for the Church in various lands and nations to be deprived of communication with each other. It is accordingly absurd to assert that it is necessary for the Mass to be celebrated in the local vernacular languages.

The second argument for the use of Latin is that all reason and propriety demands that in the sacred rites, great reverence and dignity be exhibited. And the sacrifice of the Mass is the most supreme of all sacred rites and the primary form of divine worship. Therefore it is fitting that the very highest degree of care and vigilance be exercised that it is always celebrated with the greatest possible reverence and dignity. Now, if it were necessary that the Mass were always to be celebrated in the vernacular tongue, this reverence and dignity would be gravely imperiled, and, indeed, could hardly be consistently preserved. This would result from the coarseness and crudity of irreligious persons amongst the congregation. Such persons, wholly lacking in devotion and piety, would come to regard this venerable Sacrament with less awe. Indeed, this could soon become an impious overfamiliarity and even contempt. For this reason, sound judgment dictates that it is not beneficial for the Mass to be said in the vernacular language, as a usual practice.

The third argument rests upon the fact that the use of Latin is the ancient, time-honored, and unvarying practice and tradition of the Western Church. This is very clearly demonstrated by the writings of innumerable ancient authors, such as Saint Isidore [of Seville],[28] Alcuin,[29] Amalarius,[30] and many others. These authors offer irrefutable testimony that Latin was then employed in sacred liturgies throughout Spain, France, Germany, and other parts of Europe. Now, at the time at which such authorities were writing [i.e., the early Middle Ages], Latin had already long ceased to be the vernacular language. And in defense of this well-established practice and norm, the Council of Trent expressly prohibited the celebration of the Mass in vernacular languages.

I have said that the use of Latin in the Mass arises from the ancient custom and practice of the Western Church. This, indeed, was the vernacular language at the time of the establishment of this Western Church. For in the Greek Church, a similar practice exists in their use of Greek in the liturgy. [That is to say, the idiom of Greek used in liturgy was the vernacular idiom in

---

[28] Saint Isidore of Seville (c.560–636) served as archbishop of Seville for over thirty years. He had a reputation of being one of the most learned men of his times.

[29] Blessed Alcuin of York (724–804) was an English monk and pupil of Saint Bede the Venerable. He served as tutor and advisor to the emperor Charlemagne.

[30] Amalarius (c.755–c.850) was a French bishop who left some of the earliest detailed descriptions of the celebration of the Mass.

the earliest years of the Greek Church but is no longer the everyday form of the language.] Similarly, those in Syria use the archaic Chaldean language. These ancient idioms are retained in the liturgy, though now they are understood only by a minority of learned people. The language used is not the vernacular, but it remains a common language of cultural identity and is generally known by the more educated classes. A similar situation is also found in the Arabian Churches in several Eastern regions. The form of Arabic in general, colloquial use is one thing, but the form of Arabic which priests employ in celebrating the divine liturgy is quite another. Here the reader is referred to the work of Saint Robert Bellarmine, *On the Sacraments in Kind*, Book 2, chapter 31.

At this point, the objector[31] to the Latin Mass may point out that some eight centuries ago it was granted by the apostolic see that the divine liturgies could be celebrated in the Slavonic language for people in those regions. The objector may argue, therefore, that it is quite possible for permission to be granted to other nations that they should similarly celebrate the Mass in their own vernacular languages.

On this issue, there are several important distinctions to be made. First, I acknowledge that the Church is indeed able to permit the vernacular language to be used

---

[31]   In the Latin text of this essay, the second person is used here ("You may say…"). However, this use of the second person is simply a conventional literary device for framing and responding to possible objections. The translation has been adjusted to make this clear.

in the celebration of the liturgy, exercising prudence and right judgment, in cases where there is some urgent or grave cause. But I deny the conclusion that such permission may, or should, be extended more generally and broadly. There were particular, compelling reasons why the supreme pontiff granted permission for the sacred liturgies to be celebrated in the Slavonic language. These are described by Aeneas Silvius [Piccolomini][32] in chapter 13 of his *Historia Bohemica*. At that time, the entire kingdom of the Slavs embraced Christianity together. As a result, it was then simply not possible to find a sufficient number of men who could serve as priests who were capable of celebrating the holy Mass in Latin. Therefore it seemed better to the apostolic see, and more consistent with the will of God, that the holy sacrifice of the Mass should be celebrated in the Slavonic language rather than that it should not be celebrated at all.

But, in the course of time, these Slavonic lands moved from their earlier primitive and barbaric condition to a more cultured and educated state, and more and more candidates for the priesthood emerged with sufficient expertise in Latin. The use of the Slavonic language in liturgy then ceased. They then began to conform with the general practice of the entire Western Church— namely, of using Latin in the celebration of the Mass. And this practice continues there till the present day.[33]

---

[32] Aeneas Silvius Piccolomini, who became Pope Pius II in 1458.

[33] The variety of languages and rites in use in the Christian Churches in Eastern Europe are diverse and complex at the present

Second, the objector may cite the apostle [Saint Paul], contending that he instructs that the public prayers and readings of the Church should be said in the vernacular tongue, when he writes in 1 Corinthians 14: "If the trumpet sounds an uncertain note, who shall prepare themselves for battle? And similarly, if you speak with a tongue which is not comprehensible, how shall the assembly know what it is which is being said? You will be talking, so to speak, to the air!"

But the apostle is not referring here to the reading of Sacred Scripture nor to the prayers of the divine liturgy itself. Rather he is referring to exhortations, homilies, and sermons. Testimony to this interpretation of Saint Paul's words is offered by Saint Cyprian, Saint Basil, and Saint Ambrose.

These witnesses are all cited by [Saint Robert] Bellarmine in Book 2, chapter 16, of his work *On the Word of God*. He shows that from the earliest times in the Church, the faithful gathered together regularly. And at

---

time, reflecting the schism between Rome and Constantinople, as well as the influence of the Protestant schism. Both the Roman (Latin) Catholic rite and the Byzantine (Greek) Catholic rite continue to flourish, as well as various Orthodox churches (in communion with Constantinople, but not in communion with Rome). In addition, many churches continue to use Old Church Slavonic (the language used at the time of Methodius and Cyril, but no longer a vernacular idiom). The author here is clearly referring to the Roman Catholic churches in the Slavonic nations, who adopted Latin as the language for the celebration for the Mass as soon as a sufficient number of educated and literate priests were available.

these gatherings, firstly—as testifies Saint Justin [Martyr] in his *Apologia*—the Sacred Scriptures were read, hymns of devotion were sung, and the presiding bishop would then deliver a homily or exhortation to the congregation. Following this, the sacred mysteries of the Mass were celebrated. Now, at the time when Saint Paul was writing to the Corinthians, there were many who wished to make an ostentatious display of their gift of tongues, and would speak in incomprehensible words [either in the form of glossolalia or unknown dialects]. And it was these whom he was endeavoring to correct when he instructs that sermons and exhortations be delivered in languages which were able to be understood by all.

Third, the objector to the use of Latin in the Mass may cite Pope Innocent III and his decree *Quoniam in plersique de officio judicis ordinarii* [which emerged from the Fourth Lateran Council]. In this decree, the pontiff instructs that in cities in which a mixture of languages were in use, the local bishop should take care to provide suitable men [to exercise the sacerdotal ministry]. These men should be competent to celebrate the divine liturgy and to administer the sacraments to people speaking the different languages in use.

But in this decree, Innocent [III] was referring only to the Greek and Latin liturgical idioms when he speaks of a "mixture of languages." Indeed, at the time in which he was writing,[34] a large portion of Greek Constantinople

---

[34] 1215.

was in the hands of members of the Latin Church. In the [Fourth] Lateran Council, which was convened by the Western Church, a great many Greeks also attended. These [Greek-speaking Catholics] requested that in localities in which there was a mixture of Catholics of the Roman [Latin] and Byzantine [Greek] rites, two bishops should be appointed—one for the Latin rite, and one for the Greek rite. But the holy synod and the pope declared that such a step was neither fitting nor prudent since it would mean that two bishops would be deputed to govern one diocese and one particular church. Rather, the one bishop should exercise pastoral solicitude to ensure that there were sufficient sacred ministers competent to celebrate the divine liturgies and administer the sacraments to all the faithful in the appropriate language—meaning, to Catholics of the Latin rite, in the Latin language, and to Catholics of the Byzantine rite, in the Greek language.

Considering properly the specific context and intention of the decree of Pope Innocent III, it must be obvious to all that he was not here speaking about the celebration of the Mass or other sacred rites in the vernacular languages [since neither Latin nor liturgical Greek were vernacular languages at that time]. Instead, he was extending permission and declaring his wish for Catholics of the Byzantine rite to celebrate the liturgy using the Greek language, even if they are in a territory in which the Latin rite is prevalent; and, conversely, for Catholics of the Latin rite to celebrate the liturgy using the Latin language, even when in territories in which the Greek rite is prevalent. This commendable practice continues to be permitted by the Church even in the present day.

Fourth, the objector to the Latin Mass may assert that the principal purpose of divine liturgy is the instruction and consolation of the people, but the people are not able to be instructed or consoled by a liturgy which is conducted in a language they do not understand. Therefore (to continue this line of reasoning) it is preferable for the Latin language, which is unknown to the majority of the population, not to be used in the celebration of the Mass.

In this instance, I must deny the premise. For the true objective of the divine liturgy is *not*, in fact, the instruction and consolation of the people but rather the worship and honor of God by the Church! These acts of worship and honor are fittingly conducted with the highest possible degree of dignity, gravity, beauty, and majesty. And there is no doubt that the splendor and mystery of these sacred rites should be considerably diminished were they to be conducted only in the vernacular or everyday language of the common people.

And as far as the instruction and edification of the people is concerned, this should be adequately provided by means of catechesis, homilies, sermons, and exhortations. In accordance with the directives of the Council of Trent, such instructional and hortatory material should be offered frequently by the ordained ministers of the Church in a language which is understood by the gathered faithful.

Prayer of Pope Innocent III for the Defense and Tranquility of the Catholic Church

Defend us, O Lord, we beseech thee,
from all perils of mind and body;
and, through the intercession of the blessed
and glorious Mary,
the Virgin Mother of God,
together with your blessed apostles Peter and Paul
and all your saints,
kindly grant unto us well-being and peace;
so that,
with all its external foes destroyed,
and all internal errors extirpated,
thy holy Church may serve thee
in perfect liberty and tranquility.
Through the same Christ our Lord.
Amen.